Almost Read to WRITE

Fun-filled activities and reproducibles for building early writing skills

Gross-Motor Activities
whole group • small group • centers

Fine-Motor Activities
whole group • small group • centers

Practice Pages
tracing pages • alphabet pages

Managing Editor: Kimberly Brugger-Murphy

Editorial Team: Becky S. Andrews, Diane Badden, Janet Boyce, Tricia Kylene Brown, Kimberley Bruck, Karen A. Brudnak, Kitty Campbell, Marie Cecchini, Pam Crane, Roxanne Labell Dearman, Beth Deki, Lynette Dickerson, Sue Fleischmann, Sarah Foreman, Kristin Bauer Ganoung, Deborah Garmon, Heather Graley, Tazmen Hansen, Marsha Heim, Lori Z. Henry, Lucia Kemp Henry, Debra Liverman, Dorothy C. McKinney, Thad H. McLaurin, Brenda Miner, Sharon Murphy, Jennifer Nunn, Tina Petersen, Mark Rainey, Greg D. Rieves, Hope Rogers, Andrea Singleton, Donna K. Teal, Sue Walker, Carole J. Watkins

www.themailbox.com

Manufactured in the United States
10 9 8 7 6 5 4 3 2 1

Table of Contents

Motor Activities

Practice Pages

A **pincer grip** or **pincer grasp** is the ability to hold objects between the thumb and the forefinger.

Crossing the midline is the ability to move an arm across the imaginary midline of the body.

What's Inside?

Over  80 activities!

Gross-Motor Activities

Fine-Motor Activities

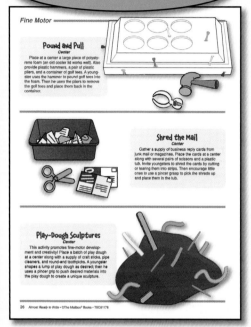

Tracing Pages PLUS Alphabet Pages

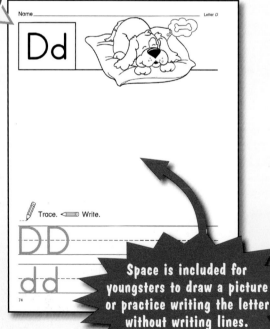

Space is included for youngsters to draw a picture or practice writing the letter without writing lines.

Gross Motor

Splashing Around
Center

Little ones splish and splash across the midline in this center. Set out a few small washcloths near your water table. A student pinches a washcloth between his thumb and index finger and dips it in the water. Then he moves his arm back and forth in a sweeping motion, touching the right and then the left side of the table with the washcloth. For a fun twist, add a few floating toys to the water and encourage him to move the toys using the washcloth.

Hip Hip Hooray
Center

Cheerleading is a fun way for little ones to practice crossing the midline. Set out a pair of cheerleader pom-poms near a full-length mirror. A student stands in front of the mirror and grips the pom-poms' handles. Then she watches herself in the mirror as she makes large arm movements, moving the pom-poms in diagonal and horizontal lines across her body.

Pool Party
Whole group

Have students sit on the floor and pretend they are in a swimming pool. Model a variety of swimming strokes that require large arm movements and crossing the midline. Invite youngsters to join in the swimming fun.

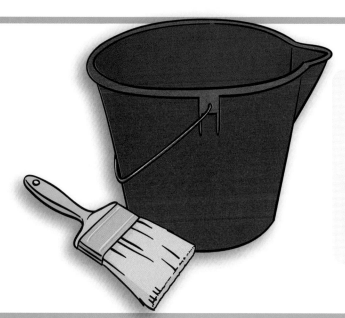

Pretend Painting
Center

For this crossing-the-midline activity, gather large paintbrushes and empty buckets or pails (paint cans). During center time, a child chooses a brush and a paint can. Then he "paints" the walls and furniture in the classroom, making sure to sweep the paintbrush diagonally and from side to side.

Prickly Letters
Center

Here's a fun way to familiarize little ones with the variety of lines used to form letters. Attach a length of Velcro fastener to your carpet in the shape of a desired letter. Encourage students to crawl along the tape, feel the prickly surface, and examine each line that forms the letter. To make a different letter, simply reposition or add to the Velcro fastener as needed.

Walk the Vine
Center

Try this unique approach to modeling handwriting strokes. Attach green electrical or masking tape (jungle vine) to the floor to make three paths: a curved path, a straight path, and a zigzag path. Also provide three jungle-themed stuffed animals. Explain that the stuffed animals need help getting to the opposite ends of the vines. A child chooses an animal and holds it while she walks the length of one vine. Then she sets the animal down and repeats the process with each remaining animal, following a different vine each time.

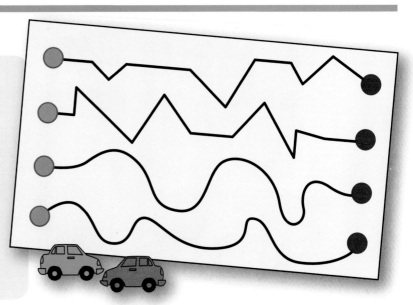

Rolling Along
Center

With this activity, students practice following lines as well as moving from left to right. Attach a length of bulletin board paper to a tabletop and draw on it several paths using straight, diagonal, and curved lines. Add a large green dot to the left side of each path and a red dot to the right side of each path. Place several toy vehicles nearby. A student chooses a vehicle and places it on a green dot. Then he rolls the vehicle along the path until he reaches the red dot.

Bubbles All Around
Whole group

Students practice crossing the midline with this bubbly idea. Play a recording of lively music as you walk around the room blowing bubbles. Invite youngsters to swing one arm at the bubbles to pop them. Repeat the activity encouraging students to use the opposite arm.

Copy Cats
Whole group

With this activity, little ones practice common handwriting strokes with whole-arm movements. Demonstrate a large arm movement, such as pointing to the ceiling and then bringing your arm straight down. Prompt students to imitate your movement while saying, "Copy cat, copy cat, we can move our arms like that!" Repeat the activity several times using a variety of arm movements.

Stretch It Out
Center

Little ones spring into action to strengthen their hand and arm muscles! Tie together the ends of a length of wide elastic and place it near a full length mirror. A student stands in front of the mirror and steps on one portion of the elastic loop with both feet. Then he pulls the opposite portion of the elastic loop above his head. He watches himself in the mirror as he moves his hands and feet to change the shape of the elastic.

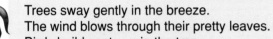

A Breezy Day
Whole group

Practice left-to-right movement and crossing the midline with this cute song!

(sung to the tune of "The Muffin Man")

Trees sway gently in the breeze.
The wind blows through their pretty leaves.
Birds build nests up in the tree.
Oh what a sight to see.

Lift arms and sway side to side.
Sweep left arm to the right and right arm to the left.
Cup hands.
Shade eyes and look to the left and then look to the right.

Bend and Touch
Whole group

This workout gives students practice crossing the midline plus the chance to get their wiggles out. Instruct each student to stand with her feet apart and then touch her left foot with her right hand. Encourage her to do the exercise several times. Then have her repeat the exercise touching her right foot with her left hand. Repeat the process having students touch each knee with the opposite hand or each knee with the opposite elbow.

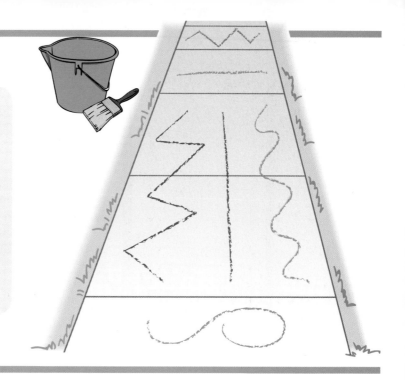

Painting With Water
Whole group

This outdoor activity is a great way for students to use whole-arm movements to practice handwriting strokes. On a sidewalk or cemented play area, use sidewalk chalk to draw large straight, diagonal, and curved lines. Set out a tub of water and a supply of wide paintbrushes. Invite each student to dip a paintbrush in the water and then have him use large arm movements to paint over the lines.

Lighting the Way
Center

This bright center idea gives little ones practice moving from left to right. On a length of bulletin board paper, draw several paths using combinations of straight, diagonal, and curved lines. Clearly mark the starting and ending points of each path. Attach the paper to a wall and set a few flashlights nearby. A student turns on a flashlight and points the beam of light at the beginning of a path. She then moves the beam along the entire length of the path. She repeats the activity with each remaining path.

Disco Dancing
Whole group

Practice crossing the midline with this classic dance move. Play a recording of disco music. Demonstrate the dance move by pointing your right arm straight up and then bringing it across the midline to point to your left foot. Invite students to join in as you replicate the move several times. Then repeat the dance move using the opposite arm.

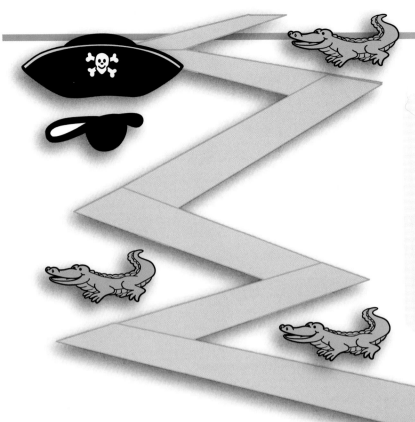

Walk the Plank
Center

This novel approach to modeling handwriting stokes is sure to be a hit with your little ones! Attach wide masking tape to the floor to create three planks: a straight plank, a curved plank, and a zigzag plank. If desired, set out a tub of pirate apparel and lay crocodile cutouts on the floor around each plank. A student puts on the desired pirate apparel and walks across each plank without falling in the water with the crocodiles.

Morning Moves
Whole group

Use this action-packed chant to wake up sleepy little ones and to practice skills such as handwriting strokes and crossing the midline.

This is the way
We warm up each day.
Touch your right foot.
Touch your left foot.
Stretch up tall.
Don't move at all.
Up and down,
From the sky to the ground.
Point over here. Point over there.
Move your arms without a care.
Crouch right down
To the ground.
Now the last—
Sit down fast.

Touch left hand to right foot.
Touch right hand to left foot.
Stretch arms high.
Freeze.
Reach up and then touch the floor.
Repeat.
Point across the midline with each arm.
Make sweeping motions with arms.
Crouch.

Stand.
Sit down.

Rhythmic Reach
Whole group

Little ones practice crossing the midline with this activity! Have youngsters sit cross-legged facing you. Then place a beanbag on the floor next to each child's right hip. Play a recording of relaxing music and instruct each child to reach across her body with her left arm, pick up the beanbag, and then bring her arm back and place the beanbag on the floor next to her left hip. Have her repeat the process using her right arm. For an added challenge, repeat the activity using a recording of upbeat music.

Invisible Paintings
Whole group

With this giggle-inducing song, students use whole-arm movements to "paint" shapes and lines.

(sung to the tune of "My Bonnie Lies Over the Ocean")

It's such fun to paint pretty pictures.	*Move right arm back and forth.*
I paint lots of circles and squares.	*Draw a circle and a square in the air.*
I paint lines both crooked and straight.	*Draw crooked and straight lines.*
I even paint big hungry bears! Grrrr!	*Arch fingers like claws.*
Painting, painting,	*Move right arm back and forth.*
I paint lots of circles and squares, and squares!	
Painting, painting,	*Move left arm back and forth.*
I even paint big hungry bears!	

Up, Down, and All Around!
Small group

For prewriting practice, program tagboard cards with arrows as shown. Position students in an open space so each child has plenty of room to move. Hold a card in the air and encourage each student to move his arm in the direction indicated by the arrow. Continue in the same way, adjusting the cards so youngsters move their arms in several directions.

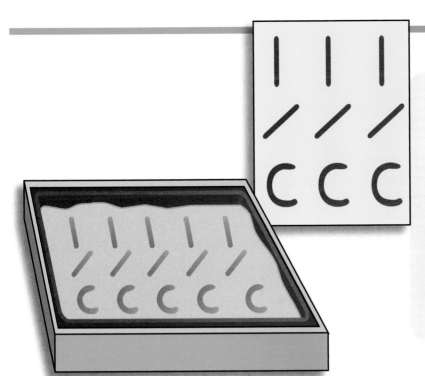

Drag the Dowel
Center

Draw diagonal lines, straight lines, and curved lines on a large sheet of paper and attach it to a wall near your sand table. A youngster stands at one end of the sand table. She reaches toward the opposite end of the table and places the tip of a short dowel or unsharpened pencil in the sand. Then she draws a line shown on the paper by dragging the dowel through the sand toward her body. She continues in the same way with each remaining line.

Buzzing Bees
Whole group

Youngsters build muscle strength and coordination when they sing this fun song!

(sung to the tune of "Row, Row, Row Your Boat")

Buzz! Buzz! Bumblebees
Fly from flower to flower each day.
Pick up pollen with your feet
And take it on your way.

Move arms in big circles.
Draw line from left to right in the air.
Stamp feet.
Draw zigzag lines in the air.

Windy Day
Whole group

Give each child in the group a length of wide ribbon and keep one for yourself. Tell students it is a breezy day. Then have them move their ribbons in a zigzag motion as if the ribbons are blowing in the wind. Next, inform students that the wind is blowing harder and encourage them to move their ribbons accordingly. Have students repeat the process using other writing strokes, such as vertical, horizontal, and circular lines.

Midline March
Whole group

Students perform cross-body movements during this activity! Demonstrate how to lift your right knee waist high; then touch your knee with your left hand. Repeat the process using your left knee and right hand; then encourage little ones to try the movements. After a little practice, play some upbeat music and encourage youngsters to perform the motions while traveling across the room.

Splendid Sea Stars
Whole group

Youngsters practice large writing strokes and crossing the midline as they pretend to be sea stars!

(sung to the tune of "This Old Man")

Sea stars have arms called rays,	*Hold arms out.*
And they point in many ways.	*Move arms in big circles.*
They point up and down	*Draw lines straight up and down.*
And also to the side.	*Swing arms from side to side.*
Sea stars are found far and wide.	*Point to the left and then to the right.*

Brilliant Beams
Small group

Little ones use beams of light to follow lines found in letters! Have several students lie on their backs. Give each child a flashlight; then turn out the lights. Shine a beam of light in one corner of the ceiling. Encourage each youngster to shine her flashlight in the same spot. Then challenge her to follow your beam of light as you move it diagonally across the ceiling to the opposite corner. Continue in the same way with other lines found in letters, such as circles, straight lines, and zigzag lines.

Light as a Feather
Whole group

Encourage coordination and fine-motor control with this nifty idea! Give each youngster a craft feather. Instruct him to place the feather on top of his left foot. Have him lift his foot off the floor and remove the feather using his right hand. Then have him place the feather on his right foot, lift his foot off the floor, and remove the feather with his left hand. Have him repeat the process several times.

Wormy Letters
Whole group

With this cute poem, little ones form the letter *A* using large arm movements. If desired, alter the poem for use with other letters.

Three little worms decided to make	*Wiggle three fingers.*
Some wormy letters one day.	
Two slanted outward,	*Draw two slanted lines.*
The other stretched across them,	*Draw a horizontal line.*
And together they made the letter *A*.	

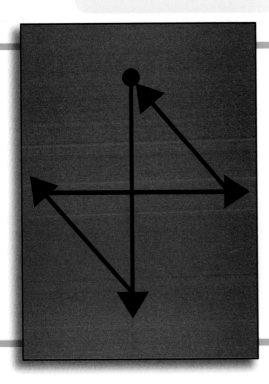

Concert Conductor
Small group

To develop shoulder stability, give each child in a small group a jumbo craft stick to use as a conductor's baton. Play a recording of music and have youngsters follow along as you demonstrate the conducting pattern shown.

Tic-Tac-Toe
Whole group

Youngsters practice letter formation with a unique twist on a favorite game! Draw a tic-tac-toe grid on your board. Invite a volunteer to choose a space on the board. Write the letter *X* in the space; then lead the group in drawing a supersize letter *X* in the air. Repeat the process with the letter *O*. Continue in the same manner until the board is complete or one of the letters emerges a winner!

Abracadabra!
Whole group

Here's a prewriting activity that will have your youngsters asking to join the fun! Hold up a letter card. Then lead students in reciting the chant shown, prompting them to use craft stick wands to draw the letter in the air after the third line. When the chant is finished, make the card disappear with great dramatic flair!

Abracadabra,
The letter [D] is here.
First, we write it;
Then we make it disappear!

Walk the Lines
Center

Students get their whole bodies moving with this engaging idea! Attach masking tape to the floor to make a supersize letter. Invite a student to walk, crawl, or hop along the letter. Encourage him to notice each line as he moves across the letter.

Fine Motor

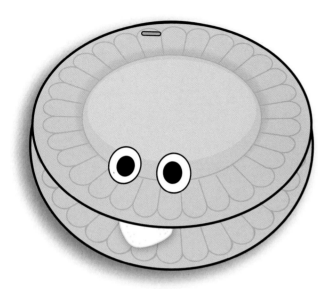

Pleasing Pearls
Small group

Staple a pair of pink paper plates, as shown, so they resemble an oyster. To give the oyster personality, attach eye cutouts to the top plate. Mix iridescent glitter with white play dough and place it at a table. Then gather several children at the table. Have youngsters pinch small amounts of play dough and roll them into balls. Then have them place the resulting pearls in the oyster.

Pencil Practice
Center

Little ones strengthen their pencil grips with this nifty idea! Place a shallow layer of sand in a tray and place the tray at a center along with fat and regular-size unsharpened pencils. A youngster holds a pencil using the appropriate grip and draws designs in the sand.

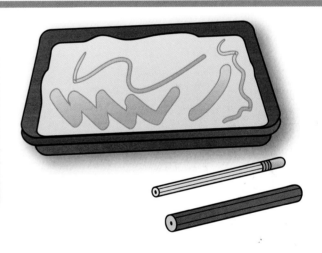

Green, Green Grass
Center

Place at the center lengths of green construction paper. Also provide scissors, glue, crayons, and sheets of drawing paper. A child gives her fine-motor skills a workout by fringe-cutting a length of green paper so it resembles grass. Then she attaches the grass to a sheet of drawing paper and adds to her artwork as desired.

Drip, Drop
Center

Youngsters practice the pincer grip with this colorful activity! Place water in several different containers and then put them in the freezer. When the water is frozen, place the ice in a large plastic tub or your water table. (Hint: place the ice on a towel to keep it from sliding around in the tub.) Provide cups of tinted salt water and eyedroppers. A youngster fills an eyedropper with water and then releases the water over the ice. What beautiful colors!

Play Dough Snip
Center

Place at the center a supply of play dough and scissors. A child grasps a ball of play dough and rolls it into a rope. Then he uses scissors to snip the rope of play dough into small pieces. He then forms the play dough into a ball again.

Lots of Legs
Center

Make a simple tagboard caterpillar cutout similar to the one shown. Then laminate the caterpillar for durability and place it at a center along with a supply of spring-style clothespins. A youngster attaches the clothespins to the caterpillar so they resemble legs and antennae.

Sponge Squeeze
Center

This water table activity is a fun way for students to build hand strength. Float a supply of sponges in your water table and set a small plastic container near the table. A child removes a sponge and squeezes the water into the container. She continues to remove and squeeze the sponges until the container is almost full. Then she pours the water back into the water table.

Weather Changes
Whole group

Little ones exercise their fingers and hands with this cute song.

(sung to the tune of "I'm a Little Teapot")

Look up in the sky. The clouds are gray.
It will be a rainy day.
But when the rain ends the sun will shine,
And the day will be just fine.

Point upward.
Wiggle fingers downward.
Open and close hands slowly.
Two thumbs up!

SQUISH, SQUISH!

Play Dough Pinch
Whole group

For each child, place two small primary-colored play dough balls in a resealable plastic bag. Give a student a bag and instruct him to pinch, squeeze, smash, and squish the two balls together to form one ball in a secondary color.

Bursting Bubbles
Center

Youngsters pop into this teacher-directed center to practice their pencil grips. In a shallow pan, put liquid dish soap and a small amount of water. Blow into the water and soap mixture with a straw to create a mound of bubbles. A child holds a straw in the same way he should hold a pencil. Then he pokes each bubble to pop it. He continues until all the bubbles have been popped.

Little Spider
Whole group

The following rhyme helps youngsters build strength in their fingers.

Little spider, climb the wall.
Watch out now! Don't you fall!
Spin a web all around,
In the air and on the ground.

Open and close hands several times.
Wiggle fingers downward.
Draw circles in the air with index fingers.
Draw circles up high; then draw circles down low.

Stormy Skies
Whole group

Here's a quick activity to help little ones form diagonal lines, which are found in many different letters! Demonstrate how to draw a bolt of lightning by making a zigzag line on your board. Then give each student a large sheet of black construction paper and a white crayon. Instruct her to cover her paper with lightning bolts.

Pinch, Squeeze, Squish
Whole group

Help students strengthen the muscles in their little hands with this quick idea. Give each student a ball of play dough. Play a recording of upbeat music and invite her to squeeze the play dough to the beat of the music. When one song is finished, invite her to roll the play dough back into a ball and then repeat the process with the opposite hand.

In the Garden
Whole group

Little ones find some fun finger exercises in this song.

(sung to the tune of "The Itsy-Bitsy Spider")

I ran out to the garden	*Run in place.*
To see what I could find.	*Point to eyes.*
I picked some sweet ripe berries,	*Pinch thumb and pointer finger together to "pick" berries.*
One of every kind.	*Hold up fingers counting to three.*
I saw a rabbit nibbling	*Hold fingers near mouth and wiggle them quickly.*
Some fresh green lettuce there.	*Continue nibbling motion.*
Then it saw me and it ran,	*Point to self.*
For I gave it quite a scare.	*Look surprised and put hands on face.*

Give It a Squeeze
Whole group

Strengthen the muscles in your little ones' hands with this simple rhyme. Display a copy of the rhyme below and teach it to your students. Then distribute small foam balls to students and have them hold the balls in their dominant hands. Invite them to recite the rhyme with you and squeeze the balls each time they say a boldfaced word. Recite the rhyme again, with students using their nondominant hands to squeeze the balls.

One, two, three, **squeeze.** Squeeze that ball now if you **please!**
One, two, three, **squeeze.** I can squeeze a ball with **ease.**
One, two, three, **squeeze.** Getting stronger is a **breeze.**

Crumpled Prints
Center

For this hand-strengthening activity, stock your art center with several shallow containers of paint, used copy paper, and a supply of white construction paper. A student crumples up a sheet of copy paper. She grips the crumpled paper in her hands and dips it in the paint. Then she presses the makeshift stamp on her paper to make a print. She repeats the process with the other containers of paint.

Suzie Q, why I declare,
Look at all your curly hair!
It's so lovely. It's so fine.
How I wish that hair were mine!

Lovely Curls
Whole group

Students practice making curving lines with this zany art activity. Give each student a large sheet of paper programmed with a face and the poem shown. Read aloud the poem. Then instruct students to make Suzie's curly hair by drawing curlicues all around her face.

Anchors Aweigh!
Center

Build hand strength with this fun water activity. Float a few plastic boats in your water table. Fill small squeeze bottles with water and place them near the water table. A student chooses a bottle and squeezes the handle repeatedly so the stream of water hits a boat and moves it through the water.

Making Cookies
Center

This play dough center is a fabulous place for little ones to exercise their hand muscles. Set out a supply of play dough. A child rolls a handful of play dough into a ball and then uses the palm of his hand to squish the play dough into a cookie shape. He makes several cookies using one hand. Then he repeats the process with the opposite hand.

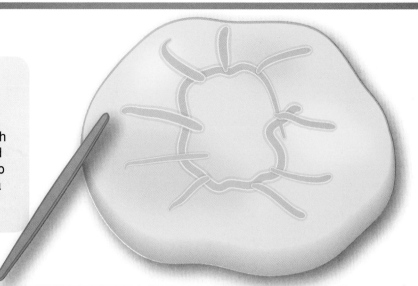

Dandy Designs
Center

Students strengthen prewriting skills with this simple idea! Place a batch of play dough at a center along with a supply of round-end toothpicks. A youngster uses his fingertips to flatten a lump of play dough; then he uses a toothpick to draw designs in the dough.

Pretty Birds
Whole group

Little ones get a fun finger workout with this adorable song!

(sung to the tune of "I've Been Working on the Railroad")

When I wake up I see many   *Stretch and wiggle fingers.*
Kinds of birds each day.   *Point to pretend birds.*
Sometimes I see fat, red robins   *Tap fingers against thumb to resemble a beak.*
Or a big, noisy blue jay. (Chee! Chee!)   *Repeat with opposite hand.*
Every day I sprinkle birdseed   *Wiggle fingers to sprinkle seeds.*
For the birds to eat.   *Repeat beak movement.*
All the birds are very happy   *Move hands as if they're wings.*
For this special treat!   *Continue moving hands.*

Faceup, Facedown
Small group

Place several playing cards faceup in front of each child. Encourage each student to use a pincer grasp to pick up a card, turn it over, and place it facedown. Have her continue in the same way with each remaining card. Have her repeat the process to return each card to its faceup position.

Foil Art
Center

Here's a simple fine-motor activity that results in a shiny modern masterpiece! Stock a center with a supply of aluminum foil sheets, construction paper, and glue. A student tears, twists, crumples, and bends pieces of foil into a variety of shapes and then glues the pieces to the construction paper until a desired effect is achieved.

Clip It!
Center

Little ones give their pincer grasps a real workout with this idea! Place at a center several clean weighted plastic containers, such as yogurt cups and margarine tubs. Also provide a supply of spring-style clothespins. (Hint: colored clothespins make this center particularly attractive for little fingers!) A youngster chooses a container and then clips clothespins around the rim. After he is finished, he removes each clothespin from the container.

Let It Rise!
Small group

Try this idea for a fine-motor workout that results in a tasty snack! Thaw a loaf of frozen bread dough and let it rise for several hours. Give each child a portion of dough. Encourage him to pinch, squeeze, press, and roll the dough; then place his individual portion of dough in a muffin cup sprayed with vegetable spray. Allow the dough to rise again; then bake it until the rolls are done. Finally, provide each child with a plastic knife and access to butter and jam. Invite him to spread a topping of his choice on his roll and enjoy!

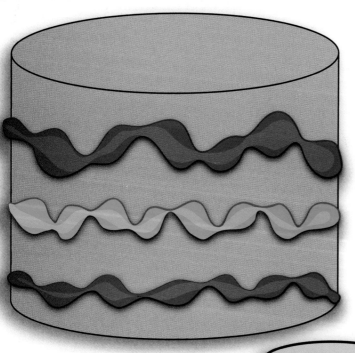

Fancy Frosting
Center

Make several large colorful cake cutouts. Then laminate each cutout to make a nonstick surface. Place the cake cutouts on a table along with play dough. A student rolls some play dough into a rope and then places it on the cake so it resembles a line of colorful frosting. Then he pinches the play dough at even intervals to add a unique creative touch to the frosting.

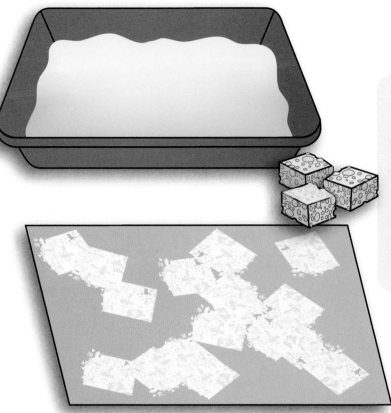

Pinch and Paint
Center

Cut a sponge into small squares. Place the sponge squares at a center along with several containers of paint in a variety of colors and a supply of construction paper. A student uses a pincer grasp to hold the sponge, dips it in paint, and then presses it on the paper. She continues in the same way until a desired effect is achieved.

Tiny Crab
Whole group

Here's a cute song that provides oodles of fine-motor fun!

(sung to the tune of "The Itsy-Bitsy Spider")

A tiny crab came swimming	*Link thumbs and wiggle fingers.*
Out of the deep blue sea.	*Make wave motions with hands.*
He crawled across the warm sand	*Quickly tap fingers on the floor.*
As proud as he could be.	*Look proud.*
I tried to pick him up,	*Pretend to pick up the crab.*
But he snapped right back at me.	*Make pincer-grasp snapping motions.*
Then he turned around and crawled back	*Link thumbs and wiggle fingers.*
Into the deep blue sea.	*Make wave motions with hands.*

Pound and Pull
Center

Place at a center a large piece of polystyrene foam (an old cooler lid works well). Also provide plastic hammers, a pair of plastic pliers, and a container of golf tees. A youngster uses the hammer to pound golf tees into the foam. Then he uses the pliers to remove the golf tees and place them back in the container.

Shred the Mail
Center

Gather a supply of business reply cards from magazines or unwanted mail. Place the cards at a center along with several pairs of scissors and a plastic tub. Invite youngsters to shred the cards by cutting or tearing them into strips. Then encourage little ones to use a pincer grasp to pick the shreds up and place them in the tub.

Play-Dough Sculptures
Center

This activity promotes fine-motor development and creativity! Place a batch of play dough at a center along with a supply of craft sticks, pipe cleaners, and round-end toothpicks. A youngster shapes a lump of play dough as desired; then he uses a pincer grip to push desired materials into the play dough to create a unique sculpture.

Clip and Pass
Whole group

Gather youngsters in a circle and give each child a plastic spring-style clothespin. Clip a clothespin to a tagboard shape and hold on to the clothespin. Demonstrate how to pass the shape by prompting the child next to you to attach her clothespin to the cutout as you unclip your clothespin. Then prompt the child to use this method to pass the cutout to her neighbor. Encourage students to pass the shape around the circle in this manner.

Beautiful Butterflies
Whole group

Imagination takes flight with this butterfly-themed song!

(sung to the tune of "If You're Happy and You Know It")

On a warm day butterflies Fly all around.	*Hook thumbs and wiggle fingers.*
They fly up and down But never make a sound.	*"Draw" a line up and then down.* *Touch finger to lips.*
They have wings that are so bright, And they sparkle in sunlight.	*Hook thumbs and wiggle fingers.* *Wiggle fingers.*
Then they fly through gardens	*Hook thumbs and wiggle fingers* *while traveling.*
And over the ground.	*Continue traveling, moving hands* *close to floor.*

Trace, Tear, Crumple
Center

Here's a fine-motor workout with a three-dimensional effect! Stock a center with large simple stencils, construction paper, old magazines, pencils, and glue. A child chooses a stencil and traces it on a sheet of paper. Then she tears a strip from a magazine page, crumples it, dips it in glue, and then presses it onto the paper inside the tracing. She continues in the same way until the outline is filled with crumpled paper.

Laundry Day
Center

Hang a makeshift clothesline in your classroom. Place a laundry basket filled with doll clothes and a supply of pinch-style clothespins nearby. A youngster uses the clothespins to clip the items to the clothesline.

More Peas, Please!
Small group

Laminate each of several green construction paper peapod cutouts. Place the peapods at a center along with a batch of green play dough. Invite a child to pinch off a small amount of play dough, roll it into a ball, and then place the resulting pea on the peapod. Encourage him to continue making peas to place on the peapod.

Straight Up!
Center

Help little ones develop shoulder stability and posture control in addition to fine-motor skills! Instead of placing paper on a tabletop, attach a large sheet of paper to your board or a wall. Provide access to materials such as crayons, markers, and chalk. A student uses the tools to draw, color, or write on the paper.

Puffy Lines
Whole group

Students practice making letter lines with this tactile idea! Draw on separate large cards the following lines: vertical, horizontal, diagonal, curved, and zigzag. Give each child a sheet of construction paper and a supply of pom-poms. Hold a card in the air; then encourage each child to arrange several pom-poms on his paper so they resemble the line shown. Have him remove the pom-poms and continue with each remaining card.

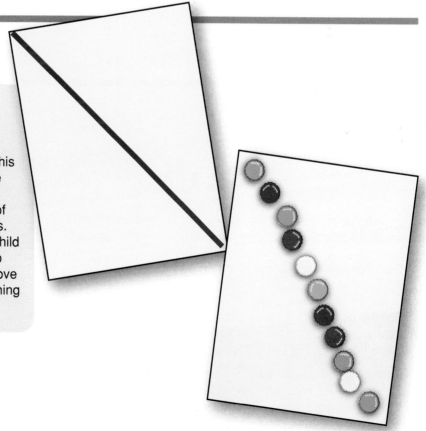

Ice Fishing
Center

Youngsters can develop strength, stability, and mobility in their hands with this fun idea! Add several ice cubes to the water in your sensory table. Place a bucket and several pairs of tongs nearby. A student uses a pair of tongs to grasp an ice cube; then she transfers the ice cube to the bucket. She continues in the same way to catch the remaining ice cubes before they melt!

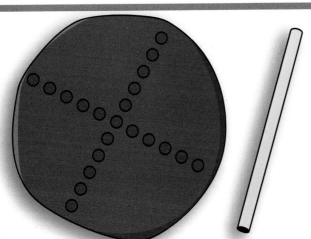

Pretty Patterns
Small group

Give each student a lump of play dough and a plastic drinking straw. Have him use the palms of his hands to flatten the dough and then use his fingertips to mold the play dough into a pancake. Next, have him grasp the straw and press the tip into the dough several times to create a unique pattern.

Make a Pie
Whole group

Lead youngsters in pantomiming the steps shown to make a pretend apple pie. What an imaginative fine-motor workout!

Grasp and pick apples from the tree; then wash them.
Peel and slice the apples.
Press the dough into a disk.
Roll the dough with a rolling pin and place the dough in a pie plate.
Put the apples in the plate and add cinnamon and sugar.
Bake the pie.

From Left to Right
Whole group

Little ones will be eager to write after singing this motivational tune! As you lead youngsters in singing the song, encourage them to move their hands from left to right, feeling the beat of the song as they write in the air.

(sung to the tune of "The Itsy-Bitsy Spider")

We are getting ready
To learn how to write.
First, we take a pencil
And go from left to right.
We'll make a new letter.
We'll learn some new words too.
Writing is the greatest—
It's so much fun to do!

Disappearing Strokes
Center

Youngsters practice making the lines found in letters and then they watch the lines disappear! Draw several different line strokes on separate paper strips. Place the strips at a center along with small chalkboards and a shallow container of water. A student chooses a strip. He dips his index finger in the water and then uses it to copy on a chalkboard the line strokes on the strip, reapplying water to his finger as needed. Once the lines are complete, he gently blows on the chalkboard and watches the lines disappear!

Cherry Picking
Small group

Put at a center a tree cutout, a plastic bowl, and a pair of tongs. Place several red pom-poms (cherries) on the tree. A student uses the tongs to pick a cherry from the tree; then she transfers the cherry to the bowl. She continues picking cherries until the tree is empty and the bowl is full!

Cooperative Lacing
Small group

Gather youngsters in a small circle and give each student a large lacing bead. Pass to a child a lace with a bead tied to one end. Encourage her to string her bead onto the lace and then pass the lace to the child sitting next to her. Have students continue in the same manner until each child has added a bead to the lace. If desired, have students continue to add beads.

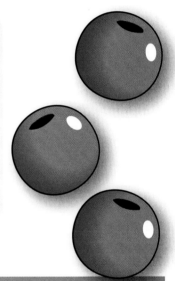

Smiley Face
Center

Students practice their pincer grips and exercise hand muscles with this cute project! Make a large smiley face on a sheet of yellow bulletin board paper and attach the paper to a table. Provide black tissue paper squares and a shallow pan of glue. A child crumples a square of tissue paper and then holds it in a pincer grip as she dips it in the glue. Then she presses it onto the facial features of the smiley face. Students continue to add tissue paper until the features are covered.

Magnetic Paths
Center

Little ones will have lots of fun following these prewriting pathways! Tape a sheet of bulletin board paper to a tabletop. Draw on the paper several different lines found in letters, such as vertical lines, horizontal lines, diagonal lines, and curved lines. Place a magnetic wand at the table along with a smooth-edged metal lid from a container of frozen juice concentrate. A student places the lid at the beginning of a line. Then she uses the magnetic wand to drag the lid along the length of the line. She repeats the process with the remaining lines.

Sleepy Bears
Small group

This cuddly idea is full of fine-motor fun! Give each child a six-section sanitized foam egg carton, six bear manipulatives, and a pair of tongs. Begin by telling youngsters that it's naptime for the bears. Encourage each child to use his tongs to pick up and place each bear in a different section of the carton (cave). After a short bear nap, have students pick up each bear with the tongs to remove it from the cave.

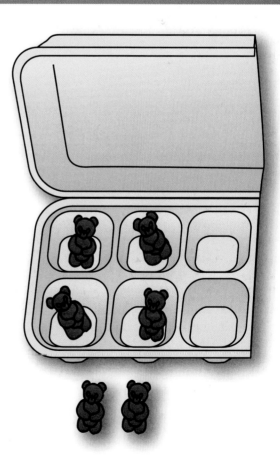

Punch and Stick
Center

Youngsters get plenty of hand and finger strengthening with this crafty idea! Place in a center a supply of colorful paper scraps, a variety of paper punches, and eight-inch squares of clear Con-Tact covering. A youngster uses the paper punches to create a supply of shapes and dots. Then he removes the backing from a Con-Tact paper square, with help as needed. He puts the square on the table sticky-side up and then presses the shapes and dots on the covering until a desired effect is achieved.

Topsy Turvy
Small group

This idea puts a real spin on using a pincer grasp! Give each child a tray along with a toy spinning top. Demonstrate for youngsters how to use a pincer grasp to hold and spin a top. Then encourage each child to hold the top as demonstrated and give it a spin!

Curved Lines
Center

At this center, youngsters practice making curved lines and create an artistic masterpiece! Have each child use brightly colored crayons to scribble on a sheet of white construction paper. Next, have each youngster roll black paint over the paper. While the paint is still wet, give her a craft stick and encourage her to practice making curved lines in the paint, revealing the crayon underneath.

Quick Flip
Small group

Youngsters will flip for this activity that can strengthen finger muscles! For each child, place ten milk caps right-side up on a sheet of construction paper. Gather a small sand timer. To begin, turn the timer over as a signal for each child to flip all her milk caps upside down. Have youngsters stop when the timer runs out. To play again, simply have each child make sure all her milk caps are facing the same way.

Syrup Squeeze
Center

Squeezing a bottle of pretend syrup in this activity can build the small muscles needed for successful writing. In advance, make a supply of pancake cutouts labeled with desired letters. Then place the cutouts at a table. Tint the glue in a squeeze bottle with brown paint so the glue resembles syrup and then place the bottle near the pancakes. A child squeezes the syrup on a letter; then he sets his pancake aside. When the glue is dry, he runs his finger over the hardened glue.

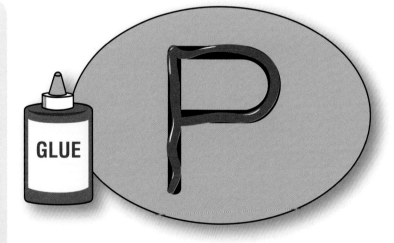

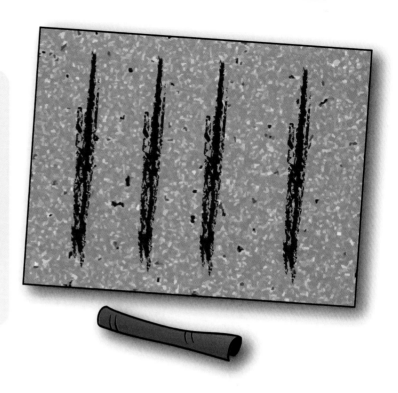

Cinnamon Sandpaper
Small group

Little ones make lines found in letters with an unusual and aromatic writing tool! Gather a small group of youngsters and give each child a sheet of sandpaper and a cinnamon stick. Demonstrate how to make a vertical line on your board. Then have each child press her cinnamon stick against the sandpaper to make several vertical lines, pausing to smell the lovely cinnamon scent. Repeat the process with horizontal and diagonal lines.

Crumple and Glue
Center

With this activity, youngsters exercise fine-motor skills and familiarize themselves with letters! Program a supply of construction paper cards with different letters. Place the letters at a center along with a supply of tissue paper squares and a squeeze bottle of glue. A child chooses a letter. He gently squeezes glue along a small section of a letter. Then he crumples tissue paper squares and presses them on the glue. He continues in the same way until the letter is covered with crumpled tissue paper.

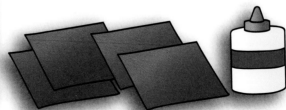

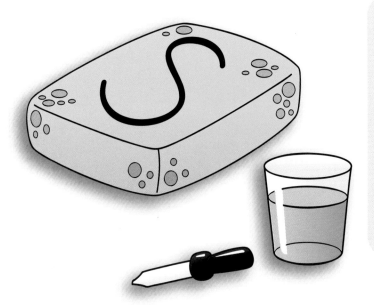

Water Lines
Small group

Little ones get lots of fine-motor practice and learn about letter formation with this unique idea! Use a black permanent marker to program each of several sponges with a different letter. Gather a small group of children. Then provide each child with a small container of water and a plastic eyedropper. To begin, demonstrate how to fill an eyedropper with water. Next, invite each child to fill her eyedropper; then encourage her to gently squeeze the top to drip water along each letter.

Sky Writing
Whole group

With this activity, youngsters practice writing skills without using paper and pencils! Give each child a plastic drinking straw. Hold a letter card in the air. Demonstrate the correct letter formation by tracing the letter with a plastic straw. Then lead each youngster in "writing" the letter in the air using her straw. When it's time to write a different letter, have each student wave her hand in the air to "erase" her practice letter!

Fingerpainted Names
Small group

Here's an idea that helps little ones form their names. Use a small paint roller to roll paint across a sheet of fingerpaint paper. Give a youngster her name card. Then help her use her finger to trace her name in the paint. If she is hesitant to touch the paint, give her a craft stick or other manipulative to use instead of her finger. If desired, roll more paint over her name and prompt her to repeat the process.

Chalky Letters
Small group

Give each child a sheet of black construction paper programmed with a letter outline drawn with white crayon. Provide a supply of colorful chalk. Model how to correctly write each letter. Then invite each youngster to write the letters several times within the outline. Encourage him to repeat the process using a variety of colors.

Mud Puddle Plunge

Trace.

Name _____

Prized Possessions

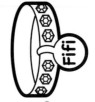

Trace.

Almost Ready to Write • ©The Mailbox® Books • TEC61178

Trace.   # Web Weavers

Name

Snacktime

Trace.

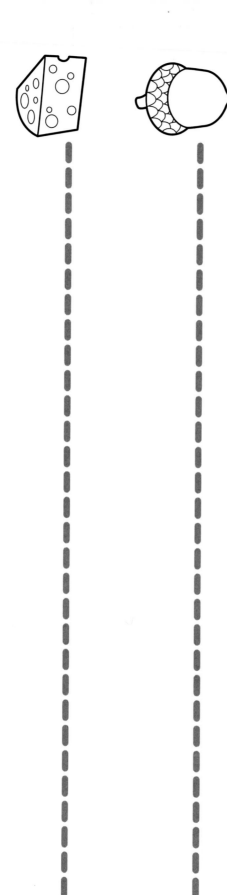
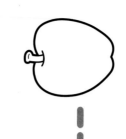

42

Name

On the "Moo-ve"

Trace.

Almost Ready to Write • ©The Mailbox® Books • TEC61178

Name _____

Trace.

Dumping Dirt

This way

Almost Ready to Write • ©The Mailbox® Books • TEC61178

Duck Stays Dry

Trace.

Name

Hop to It!

Trace.

Cute Kites!

 Trace.

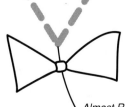

48

Cozy Campsite

Trace.

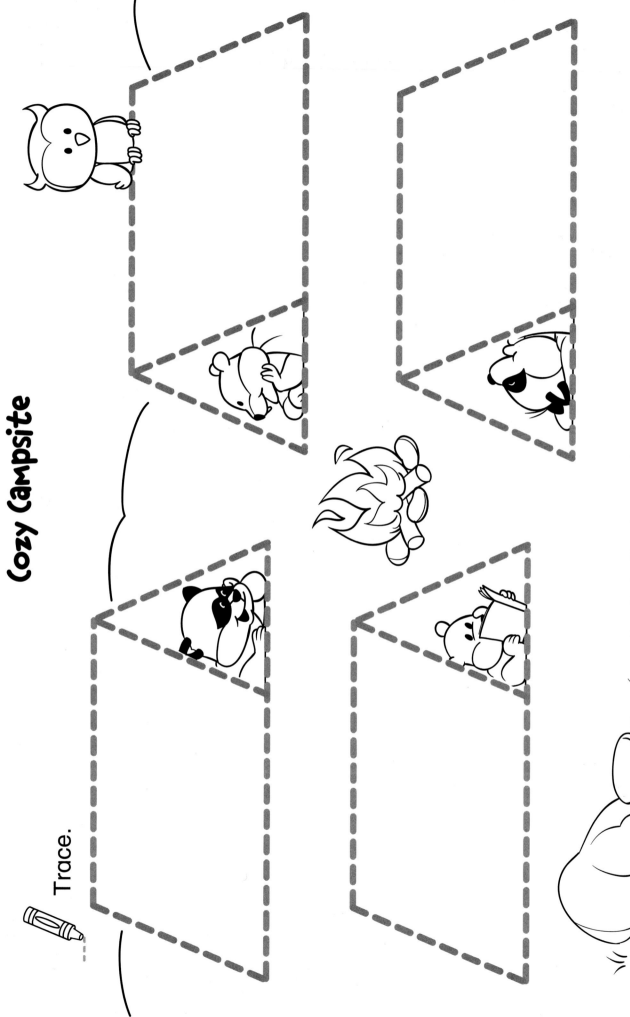

Name _____

Mole's Maze

Trace.

Name _____

High in the Sky

Trace.

Almost Ready to Write • ©The Mailbox® Books • TEC61178

Name

Penguin Play

Trace.

Score!

 Trace.

Name

Busy Bees

Trace.

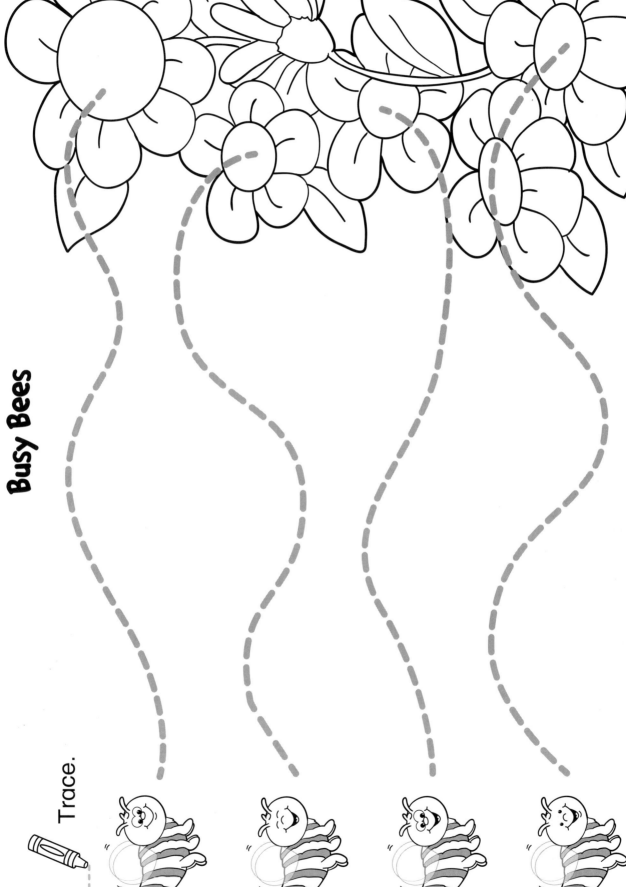

Almost Ready to Write • ©The Mailbox® Books • TEC61178

Name _____

Bubble-Blowing Bear

Trace.

Here Fishy, Fishy!

Trace.

Beautiful Butterflies

Trace.

Almost Ready to Write • ©The Mailbox® Books • TEC61178

Name _____

Going Home

Trace.

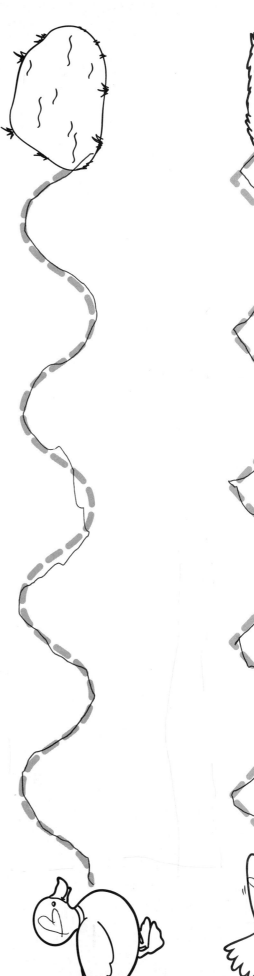

Name

Take the Cake

Trace.

Almost Ready to Write • ©The Mailbox® Books • TEC61178

Name _____

Turtle Tagalong

Trace.

Almost Ready to Write • ©The Mailbox® Books • TEC61178

Name

60

Bunny Buggy

Trace.

Name

Bath Time!

Trace.

Super Sundae!

Trace.

Name _____

Jolly Jellyfish

Trace.

Flower Friends

Trace.

Almost Ready to Write ©The Mailbox® Books • TEC61178

Name

You've Got Mail!

Trace.

MAIL

U.S. MAIL

Almost Ready to Write • ©The Mailbox® Books • TEC61178

Name

Mouse's Masterpiece

Trace.

Name

Peaceful Pond

Trace.

Breakfast Buddies

Trace.

TOASTED OATS

Name _____

Hen's Laundry Line

Trace.

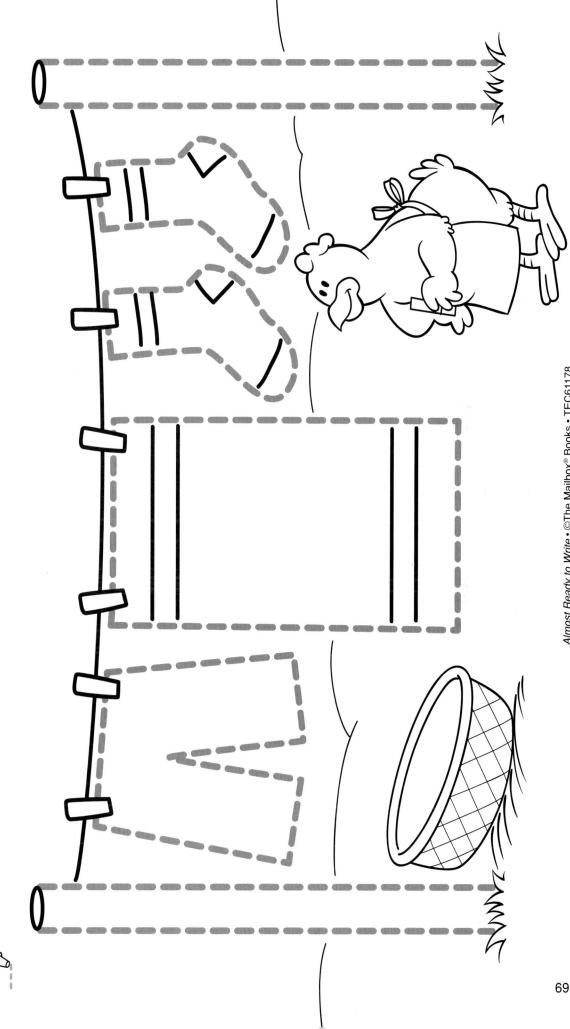

Cleaning Time!

Trace.

Almost Ready to Write • ©The Mailbox® Books • TEC61178

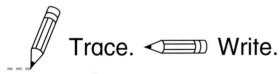 Trace. 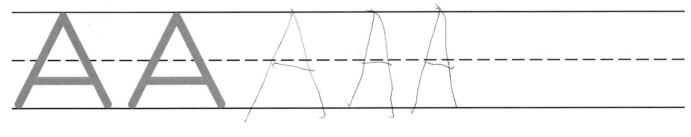 Write.

B b

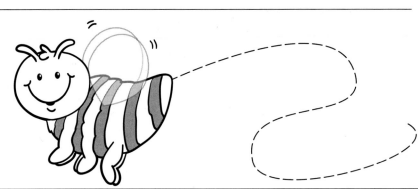

 Trace. Write.

B B

b b

 Trace.  Write.

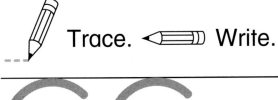

D d

Trace. Write.

D D

d d

E e

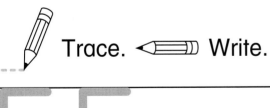
Trace. 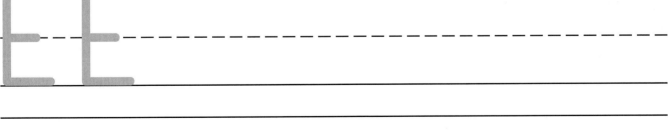 Write.

E E -

e e -

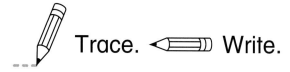 Trace. 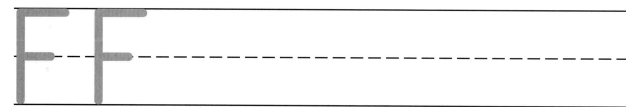 Write.

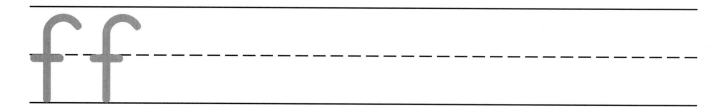

G g

 Trace.  Write.

G G

g g

H h

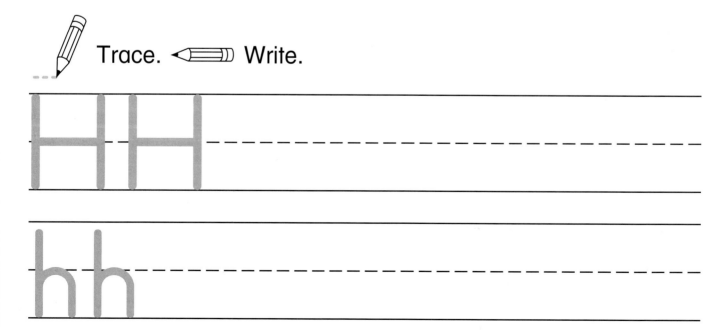

Trace. ◁▭▭ Write.

H H H -

h h -

Trace. ◁▭▭ Write.

I I

i i

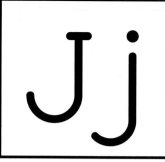

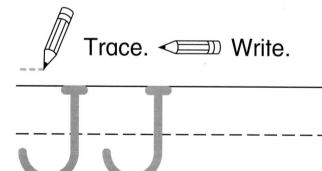 Trace. Write.

J J J

j j j

Almost Ready to Write • ©The Mailbox® Books • TEC61178

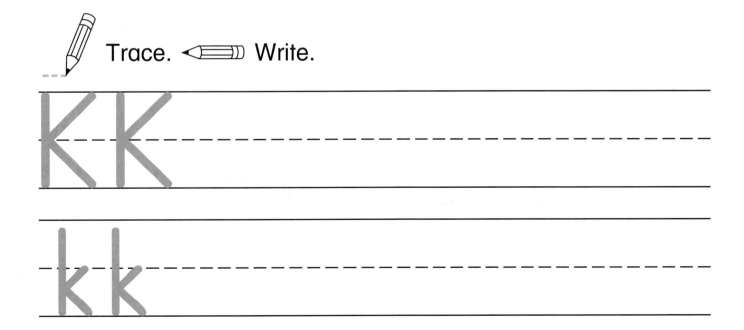

Trace. Write.

L l

Trace. ◁▭▭ Write.

L L

l l

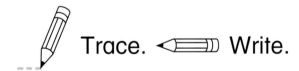 Trace. 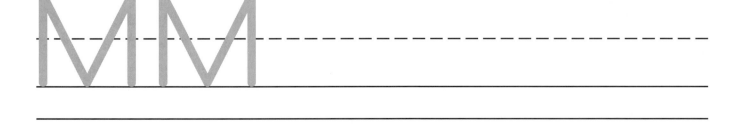 Write.

N n

 Trace.  Write.

N N

n n

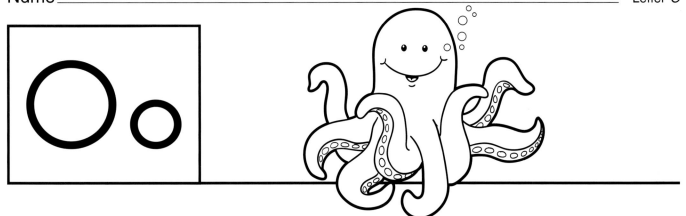

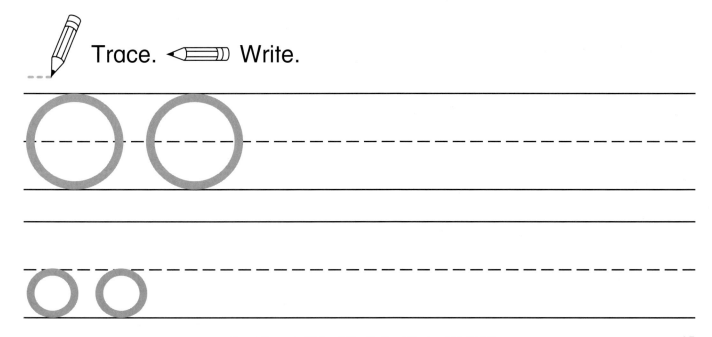

Trace. Write.

Pp

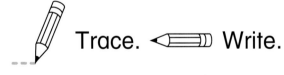 Trace. Write.

P P

p p

 Trace. 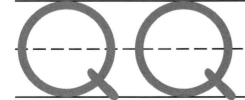 Write.

R r

 Trace. ◁▭▭ Write.

RR

r r

Almost Ready to Write • ©The Mailbox® Books • TEC61178

S s

 Trace. ◁▭▷ Write.

S S

s s

Tt

Trace. Write.

    Almost Ready to Write • ©The Mailbox® Books • TEC61178

 Trace.  Write.

V v

 Trace.  Write.

V V

V V

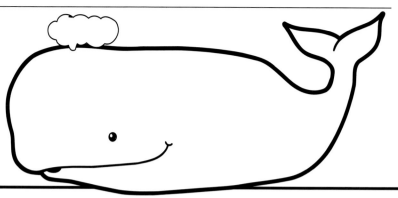

 Trace.  Write.

Name _____

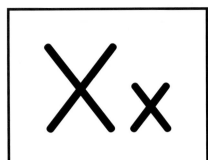 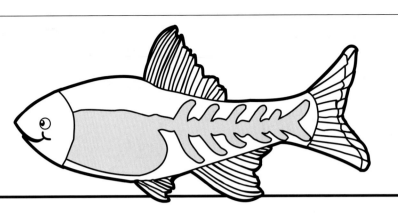

Trace. Write.

Almost Ready to Write • ©The Mailbox® Books • TEC61178

 Trace. Write.

Y   Y

y   y

Z z

 Trace. ⬤▭ Write.

Z Z

z z

Almost Ready to Write • ©The Mailbox® Books • TEC61178